50 THINGS TO TRY IN WINTER

This book belongs to:

....

Age: ....

New Year's wish: ....

....

Wishing you happy holidays, all over the world!
– Kim

Published by b small publishing ltd.
www.bsmall.co.uk

Text and illustrations copyright © b small publishing ltd. 2021

1 2 3 4 5   ISBN 978-1-912909-92-6

Text, design and illustrations by Kim Hankinson.
Editorial by Sam Hutchinson. Cover design by Vicky Barker.

Printed in China by WKT Co. Ltd.

British Library Cataloguing-in-Publication Data.
A catalogue record for this book is available from the British Library.

Activities for ...

chilling, crafting, giving, making,
wishing, wrapping, celebrating,
hibernating, ice-cool SUPERSTARS!

KIM HANKINSON

FILM
Pretend you are looking through an old-fashioned film camera!

SOUNDS LIKE

BOOK

CORRECT!

HOW TO
USE THIS BOOK

This book is full of daring-looking-thinking-listening activities everyone can try. Starting on any page, do as many activities as you can fit into a day and in any order you like.

The activities are colour-coded to help you choose what sort of activity you would like to do. Match the activity key below with the coloured circle in the contents list opposite or the coloured circle enclosing each page number. There are extra pages for notes and doodles throughout the book.

Have fun and enjoy the winter delights!

ACTIVITY KEY

EXPLORE	DARE	MAKE	CREATE	SKILLS	CAREFUL!
●	●	●	●	●	●

Always ask an adult when you see a red warning symbol.

CONTENTS CHECKLIST:

HOW MANY WORDS?
Show with your fingers.

NUMBER OF SYLLABLES
Tap arm with your fingers.

CHARADES!
Use these signals to help you mime a film or book title without talking. You have one minute. Go!

Ice name!

Write your name in one loooooooong line.
Start at the skater's blade.

Gaps in the line are jumps ... so it does
not have to be joined-up writing!

World fare

Have an international winter feast and eat some festive food. Try these or discover your own!

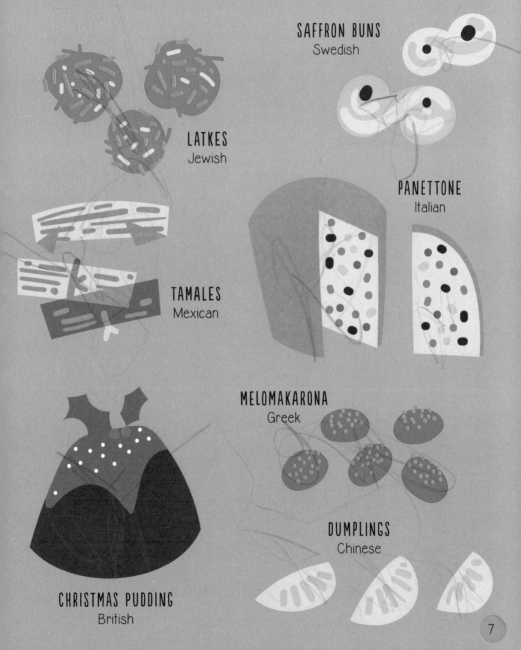

SAFFRON BUNS
Swedish

LATKES
Jewish

PANETTONE
Italian

TAMALES
Mexican

MELOMAKARONA
Greek

DUMPLINGS
Chinese

CHRISTMAS PUDDING
British

Winter wonderland

Things look different in winter.
Look out for the following objects.

STARS

CARDS

FIREWORKS

ICE RINK

DECORATIONS

LANTERNS

SNOW
(real or fake)

HANUKKAH
MENORAH

GIFTS

10 out of 10!

Practise these training positions used by figure skaters. No ice required!

SQUATS

Do these to prepare for a 'sit spin' where you squat on one leg and hold the other leg straight out in front of you! You will need very strong legs!

STAR JUMPS

Train your body for the incredible split jump, which is an extreme star jump ... on ice!

LUNGE

A lunge off the ice is pretty much the same as a lunge on the ice, just a little slower and much easier for beginners! This will help you balance.

Mug hug

Make your own super hot chocolate powder, just add dairy or nut milk.

GIFT A HUG
Use an old jar and fill it two thirds with cocoa powder, one third with sugar. Add a teaspoon of salt, mix, close tight and add ribbon!

SUGAR
3 heaped teaspoons

COCOA POWDER
1 heaped tablespoon

PINCH OF SALT

HEAT IT!
Be gentle. Do not let it boil.

WHISK IT!
This will get out all the lumps and make it super creamy.

1 MUG OF MILK
Nut milk or dairy! Either works well.

Paper snowflake

Try this awesome, one-of-a-kind
3D 'paper flake'.

2 SHEETS OF PAPER
THREAD
PENCIL
SCISSORS
GLUE

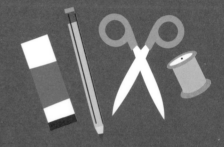

1. Make a fold at one edge of the paper. Turn the sheet over.

2. At the same end, make another fold the same depth. Repeat, turning and folding.

3. You have made a concertina! Repeat on a second sheet of paper using the first as a template to make a copy.

SIDE VIEW!

4. Each concertina should be symmetrical. If they are not, cut along one fold at one end so the ends are mirrored.

5. Take one concertina and tie a thread around the middle. Add a little tape to keep it in position.

6. Draw a pattern along one edge.

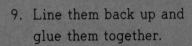

7. Cut out the design.

8. Repeat on the other concertina to make an exact copy, using your cut-out design as a template.

9. Line them back up and glue them together.

10. After the glue has dried, glue the outside edge together folding at the middle. As you do this the concertinas will open into a beautiful snowflake!

GLUE IT SO THE THREAD POKES OUT ...

HANG UP! TA-DA!

Draw a snowman based on someone you know really well.

DAILY DARE

Try out a new winter activity.

SINGING TOGETHER

SKATING
(ice or roller)

SKIING

SLEDDING

WATCHING
WINTER
SPORTS

BOWLING

Tree spotters

Go Christmas tree spotting. How many can you find?
Play with a friend and see who can spot them first.

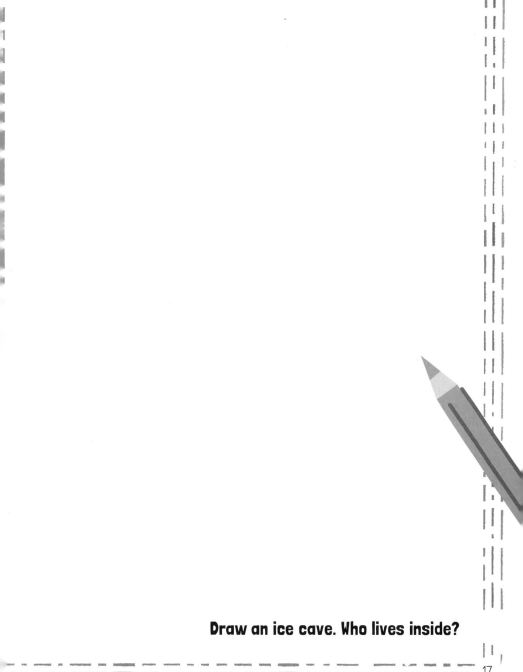

Draw an ice cave. Who lives inside?

Night light

Take pictures of outdoor lights when it is dark. Look for twinkling decorations, dazzling signs and bright shopfronts.

New hat

Spot woolly hats on other people's heads and copy the designs below. Collect as many patterns, colours and details as you can.

Where is winter?

There it is! On this page, it is snowing facts.

NIGHT-TIME, NIGHT-TIME
Places in the Arctic Circle have a polar night, where there is no daylight for a long time! One such place is Tromsø in Norway, where the darkness lasts all winter!

AMAZING ICE!
The Harbin International Ice and Snow Sculpture Festival takes place every year in China. Large blocks of ice are stacked one on top of the other to make amazing buildings. There is even an ice castle you can walk through!

CHRISTMAS MARKETS
The largest Christmas market in the world is in Vienna, Austria.

THE COLDEST CITY
About 300,000 people live in Yakutsk, Russia. It is said to be the world's coldest city. In winter, it has reached a very frosty -63°C!

FRIED CHICKEN!
In Japan, many families eat fried chicken for Christmas dinner.

BIG SKATE!
In Canada, Ottowa's Rideau Canal freezes over in winter to become the world's largest naturally frozen ice rink.

Glove it! Draw around your hand then decorate it to create your own unique glove design.

DAILY DARE

Do something nice for someone
and spread some winter cheer.

GIVE GIFTS
OR HELP WITH
WRAPPING

DECORATE

CLEAR
SNOWY
PATHS

LEND A HAND

COOK SOMETHING YUMMY

JOKES!

Learn some jokes. Or try coming up with a few of your own!

WHERE DO REINDEER DANCE?

SNOWBALLS!

FIREWORKS

SNOWFLAKE

REINDEER

TREE

WHY DO FROGS GET HOT IN WINTER?

STAR

SKI

BECAUSE THEY ARE CHRISTMAS JUMPERS!

BOBBLE HAT

Look at the winter words
or think of your own.

Do any words
have more than
one meaning?

Do they rhyme with
any other words?

Jot down anything that comes to mind.

Use rhymes or double meanings to make up a question.
The Christmas word will be the answer.

CHOIR

HOLLY

TINSEL

ICICLE

HOW DO YOU GET
AROUND IN WINTER?

SILVER

ROBIN

RIDE AN
ICICLE!

DAILY DARE

There are lots of stars to choose
from in winter. Make a wish on one!

Snowballs

Make these snowball treats.

Ask an adult!

125 G ALMOND FLOUR
375 G COCONUT FLAKES
25 G MILK (DAIRY OR NUT)
250 G HONEY

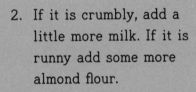

1. Put all the ingredients in a blender and mix on a low setting until it goes all doughy!

2. If it is crumbly, add a little more milk. If it is runny add some more almond flour.

3. Put the dough in a bowl. Using your (clean!) hands, take pieces and roll them into small balls.

4. Roll each ball in a little more coconut and put them in the fridge for an hour before eating. Keep any leftovers in the fridge.

Winter lanterns

Create your own paper lanterns!

1. Choose some colourful paper. Fold it in half.

2. Fold one edge back up a little and score a line.

3. Cut straight lines along the folded edge as far as the fold you made in step 2. Leave space between each cut.

4. Open the paper and lay it flat. Decorate the top and bottom with stickers and cut-out shapes.

5. Stick the edges of the paper together using glue.

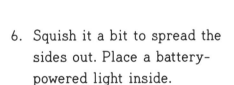

6. Squish it a bit to spread the sides out. Place a battery-powered light inside.

If you want to use a candle, place it inside a glass jar and put the jar inside the lantern to stop the lantern from catching fire.

Winter warmers

Create your own festive puppets by sewing or sticking
some simple shapes cut from felt to old socks.

RED REINDEER NOSE
Twigs make fun antler

BEAR EARS
& SNOOZY EYE

SNOWMAN HAT
& CARROT
NOSE

ROBIN BEA
& RED TUM
Use button
for eyes

Design a winter celebration card!

One of a kind

Make a unique snowflake using this mandala template.

1. Look carefully at this section.

2. Copy the first section into the one beside it. Repeat with each section until the circle is complete.

3. Now add your own details into each section in the same way.

Winter skies

Create a multicoloured winter sunset over the rooftops.

Fake it

No snow? Make some pom-pom snowballs.

YOU WILL NEED:

2 X CARDBOARD   PENCIL
SMALL PLATE   SCISSORS
GLASS   WOOL

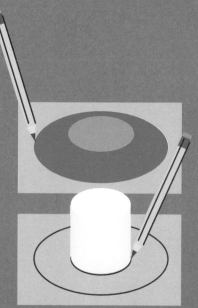

1. Draw one large and one small circle on to a piece of cardboard, as shown. Cut out. Then repeat so you have two rings.

2. Put one on top of the other and cut a slit in the side, wide enough to slide the wool through.

3. Start winding the wool around the ring. If you wind the wool back over itself, it will hold the end in place. Keep going until the ring is covered with wool.

BLIZZARD!

Have a snowball fight! Make several pom-pom snowballs or, if it has snowed, get outside!

4. Carefully cut around the edge of the wool with scissors.

5. Tie a new piece of wool around the centre, in between your card doughnuts. Tie a tight knot.

6. Gently slide the card away from each side.

7. Begin to spread the wool cut into a round shape. Trim any long or uneven bits to make the pom-pom even more round.

Snow globe

Draw your favourite winter
animal in the snow globe.

Super-sleepers

Here are a few animals that sleep right through the winter. Can you think of any more?

FAT-TAILED DWARF LEMUR

BEAR

BUMBLEBEE

TORTOISE

WOODCHUCK

SNAKE

Star crazy

Write the name of a film, game or activity. Colour in the stars to review it. Five is top points!

Name:
....

FILM OR GAME OR ACTIVITY

CIRCLE ONE ★★★★★

Name:
....

FILM OR GAME OR ACTIVITY

★★★★★

Name:
....

FILM OR GAME OR ACTIVITY

★★★★★

Name:
....

FILM OR GAME OR ACTIVITY

★★★★★

Moon gazing

Record a full Moon cycle. Draw the shape of the Moon every three or four days and write the date underneath. You will need to wait for clear skies so do not worry if you have to miss some out.

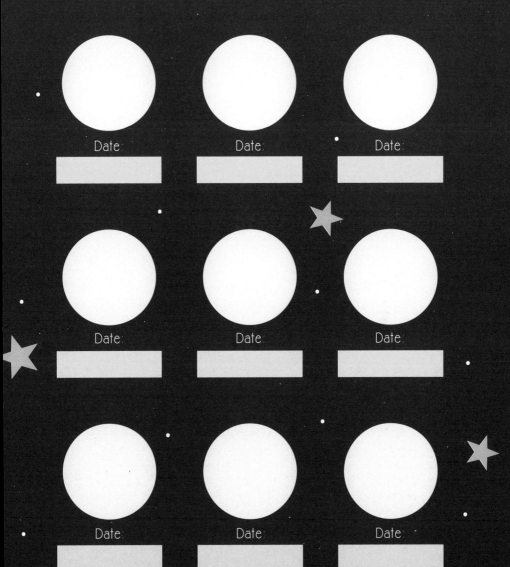

Date:

Date:

Date:

Date:

Date:

Date:

Date:

Date:

Date:

Happy New Year!

Whizz, bang, swish! Draw where you live
underneath this festive firework-filled sky.

DAILY DARE

Using your imagination, make up a story starting with ...

It was a starry winter's night ...

THINGS YOU COULD INCLUDE:

COLD MOUNTAIN

WINTER FOX

ICE CAVE

LOG CABIN

MAGIC WISH

PENGUIN

VELVET CAPE

NUTCRACKER

Solstice style

On the shortest day of the year, strange things happen in these ancient places. No one knows why!

STONEHENGE, ENGLAND

When the sun sets on the winter solstice, the rays of the setting sun line up with two important stones.

NEWGRANGE, IRELAND

Around the winter solstice, the light from the rising sun illuminates the passage and chamber of this Stone Age tomb.

MAESHOWE, SCOTLAND

As the sun sets on the winter solstice, rays of light enter the passage and central chamber of this ancient monument on Orkney.

The winter solstice is the shortest day of the year. The summer solstice is the longest day.

GOSECK CIRCLE, GERMANY

Two gates mark the position of sunrise and sunset on the winter solstice.

STONE LINES AT CERRO DEL GENTIL PYRAMID, PERU

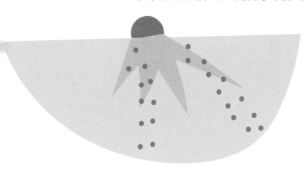

Two long lines of large rocks seem to mark a path to the pyramid here, and the sun's rays line these all up on the winter solstice!

Party hats

Make easy paper hats and decorate with winter festival-inspired touches.

Twist a piece of coloured A4 card into a point.

CONE

Stick down the edge at the join. Cut the base so it sits flat.

Put on your head to measure what length you need for a strap. Tape the elastic ends inside.

Decorate!

KING & QUEEN

Measure your head with a tape measure.

Draw a line the length of your head on a piece of card. Closer to the top edge will make a short hat, further down will make a tall hat.

FINISHING TOUCHES

POM-POM
(see page 34)

TISSUE PAPER TRIM!

ADD STARS
OR JEWEL-LIKE
STICKERS.

STREAMERS!

ow make the shape for
e top edge of the hat.
raw lines in a zigzag
or a wavy shape.

Cut out, join the ends
together and stick
with tape.

Decorate!

DAILY DARE

Think of three things you give thanks for this winter.

If you like doing this, write them down daily in a journal, or write them on pieces of paper and keep them in a jar.

Pretty silhouettes

Use long straight lines to draw wintery trees below.

Start with a thick pen for your trunk.

Use thin pens for the branches and thinner pens still for the stalks.

Use a colouring pencil to add icicles beneath the branches and snow above.

Rewind

Write down a memory from every month of the year. Look at a calendar or diary to help you remember.

JANUARY

FEBRUARY

MARCH

APRIL

MAY

JUNE

JULY

AUGUST

SEPTEMBER

OCTOBER

NOVEMBER

DECEMBER

DAILY DARE

Create some winter magic with this simple trick!

Put a coin in the palm of
one hand and show it to the
audience. Close that hand then
move both hands around.

THE TRICKY BIT

Use misdirection to stop people from seeing the magic happen. This means
distracting your audience! So pretend to cast a spell with the open hand. Use
flamboyant gestures and keep talking ... it really helps distracts the audience!

Move your hands over and
under each other.

Drop the coin through your
fingers into the open hand.

THE REVEAL

After catching the coin in your open
hand, quickly close both fists and, in
an artful manner, stop moving. Ask the
audience where the coin is!

TA-DA!

Design an epic winter lantern!

Winter wrap-up!

Make your own personal patterned paper
for wrapping up winter gifts.

STAR

TREE

TEMPLATE SHAPES

MISTLETOE

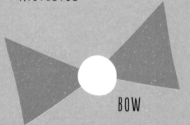

BOW

HOLLY

YOU WILL NEED:

SHEET OF CARD
PENCIL
SCISSORS
PACKING PAPER
STONES (OR SOMETHING HEAVY)
ACRYLIC OR POSTER PAINT
SAUCERS OR SMALL PLATES
SPONGES

1. Copy a shape on to card.
   Cut around the shape in a
   rectangle. Now cut the shape
   out. Fold up the edge at one
   end. Make one stencil for
   each colour you want to use.

2. Lay some packing paper flat. Weigh the corners down. Pour a small amount of each paint colour you want to use into its own saucer.

3. Dab a sponge into the paint colour you want to use first. Keep dabbing gently until the bottom of the sponge is evenly covered in paint. Not too much or too little!

4. Hold the edge of the template with one hand and lay your stencil flat against the paper. Now dab the paint on with the sponge. Do this gently. You will have to dab a few times to get an even layer.

5. Repeat to create the pattern. Do not lay your template on wet paint. Allow the artwork to dry before adding a new colour. Dry before use!

Design a festive jumper!

Mountainside

Learn to draw the mountain tops!

3. Add smaller zigzags at the back. Make sure they disappear behind the bigger triangles.

2. Draw a row of smaller triangles behind them.

1. Start with big triangles at the base of the page.

SNOW
The top of the mountain is colder, so add snow to the top.

CLOUDS
d these halfway up to show
w high the mountains are in
:omparison to the clouds.

COLOURS
Colour the first mountains with light colours and then use darker colours for the mountains that are further away.

ADD
DETAILS

DAILY DARE

Give a homemade gift to someone you like.

HAPPY
HOLIDAYS!

HAPPY
NEW YEAR!

Space spotter

Find out when you are most likely to be able to spot the International Space Station (ISS) in the sky above where you live.

The ISS is most visible in the sky at dawn and dusk. As these are not too early or late in winter, you should have lots of chances to spot it.

1. Go online and type 'spot the station' in the search bar.

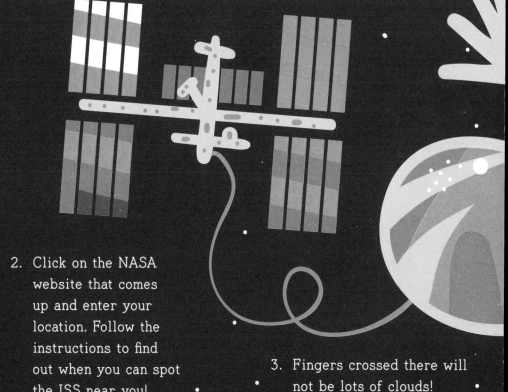

2. Click on the NASA website that comes up and enter your location. Follow the instructions to find out when you can spot the ISS near you!

3. Fingers crossed there will not be lots of clouds!

Gingerbread

Make this simple gingerbread
to share this holiday season.

YOU WILL NEED:

350 G PLAIN FLOUR
2 TSP GINGER (GROUND)
1 TSP BICARBONATE OF SODA
100 G BUTTER
175 G LIGHT SOFT BROWN SUGAR
1 EGG
3 TBSP HONEY

1. Set the oven to 190°C or
   Gas Mark 5. Put some
   greased baking paper on
   a baking tray.

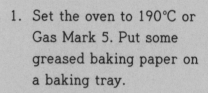

2. Put the flour, ginger and
   soda into a mixing bowl.

3. Cut the butter into squares
   and use your fingertips to
   rub it into the flour.

4. Sprinkle in the sugar and
   mix with a spoon. Then
   mix in the egg and honey.

5. Roll out to be about half
   a centimetre thick. It does
   not have to be perfect.

6. Mark the design on the dough with a toothpick.

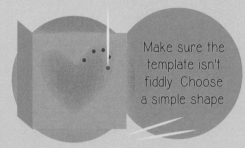

Make sure the template isn't fiddly. Choose a simple shape

7. Cut out with a butter knife and put on the tray.

8. Re-roll the extra dough and cut out more biscuits. Cook them for 15 minutes.

9. Cool on a rack. When they are cool, add icing and cake decorations!

DECORATE!

TIE IT!
Make a hole before you bake. When cooked, add a ribbon to hang it up.

ADD COLOUR
Use colourful icing.

ADD SOME SPARKLE
There are lots of fun cake decorations to try out.

Memories!

Write down the best thing that
happened this winter.

Draw something that will help you remember the memory.